This Notebook Belongs To :

D1637025

Made in the USA
Coppell, TX
29 September 2021

63154425R10069